Crystal Rae Coel, M.A.,

A WORKBOOK FOR
THE Presentation Guide Book

CUSTOMIZED FOR THE DEPARTMENT OF ORGANIZATIONAL COMMUNICATION, MURRAY STATE UNIVERSITY

Kendall Hunt
publishing company

Kendall Hunt
publishing company

www.kendallhunt.com
Send all inquiries to:
4050 Westmark Drive
Dubuque, IA 52004-1840

Contents

About the Author

D r. Crystal Rae Coel (pronounced like "Noel" but with a "C") is the Head of Elizabeth College and the Director of Speech and Debate in the Department of Organizational Communication within the Bauernfeind College of Business at Murray State University. She is the author of THE Presentation Guide Book: From the Classroom to the Boardroom and the co-author of several texts. She is also a Pennsylvania attorney and the owner of C-R-C Consulting, LLC. Dr. Coel conducts seminars within the states and overseas for Leadership, Conflict Resolution, Team Communication and the ART of Public Address.

Preface

When Aristotle defined communication as "the art of discovering in any given case the available means of persuasion," he really did mean an "art" or "craft"–not a science. In other words, he meant a practical activity where one works to shape all the elements of a presentation into one the audience eagerly accepts.

However, this is no easy task, which is why an entire academic discipline has built up around it in the past 100 years. This is also why about two dozen textbooks on the subject are available, in addition to dozens of popular books.

However, few offer the explanations, details and examples found in *A Workbook for THE Presentation Guidebook*. Specifically designed as a complement to *Selling Yourself and Your Ideas (3rd Edition)*, this workbook aims to help you construct the most difficult parts of presentations, and the most difficult presentations as well.

My hope for you is that you use this workbook to its full advantage as a supplement to existing course materials, as well as a vital complement to *Selling Yourself and Your Ideas*. We have found that success in later courses in your college curriculum is linked to your success in COM 161 Public Speaking. We are committed to assuring your success in this course and other courses. A Workbook for *THE Presentation Guide Book* Is an important component of that.

R. Michael Bokeno, Ph.D., Chair
Department of Organizational Communication
Professor and BB&T Fellow
Murray State University

Dress for Success!

Looking professional and appropriate are paramount! Make sure you understand the event and YOUR role as a presenter. Unless you are outdoors and climbing trees while you speak, you should at LEAST be in "Business Casual" attire. Otherwise, formal "Business" attire is often the preferred style when giving a presentation. Look good . . . feel good . . . BE amazing!

Business Casual Attire:

Clothing:

Men: Jackets are optional . . . Khakis, polo or dress shirts
Women: Skirts are at the knee or no more than 1 inch above the knee (mid-thigh or higher is not appropriate for the workplace) . . . Sundresses are not business casual without a cardigan sweater or a shrug

Shoes:

Closed-toe shoes for both men and women
Men: Can wear dress boots
Women: Can wear flats, dress boots or heels (Flip flops & boots with fur are not appropriate)

Accessories:

Men and Women: No visible tattoos, multiple piercings, bright nail polish, dangling or distracting jewelry . . . conservative watches for men & women are permissible

Formal Business Attire:

Clothing:

Men: Suit with a tie
Women: Conservative dress with sleeves . . . some sleeveless dresses are appropriate; otherwise it is best to have a shawl or jacket as a cover-up . . . Suit (pants or a skirt) Skirts are at the knee or **no more** than 1 inch above the knee (mid-thigh and high-thigh skirts or dresses are not appropriate for the workplace)

Shoes:

Men: Dress shoes must be polished . . . no cowboy boots
Women: Closed-toe pump with a 1-4 inch heel (flats may be worn when necessary) . . . No open-toe shoes/sandals for men or women . . . no 5 inch heels! Peep-toe shoes are fine.

Accessories:

Conservative watches are permissible for both men and women
Women: No more than 1 earring per ear
Men: No piercings unless your field recognizes the "art"
Men and Women: No visible tattoos, multiple earrings, bright nail polish
Women: Wear pearl earrings or small silver or gold earrings . . . no dangling earrings and no bracelets

THE ELEVATOR OPENING

The first 30-60 seconds of any important meeting are essential. For job placement, a potential employer is impressed or not impressed within the first few seconds or minutes of meeting an applicant. The "Elevator Opening" is your opportunity to tell the audience who you are with just a few dynamic sentences and phrases. The four core elements to include are:

- Skills
- Strengths
- Goal (s)
- Motivation

Skills

Your skills should be clear and articulated well. You should know that you are proficient with computer programs; you are an expert in auto mechanics; or perhaps you have outstanding written communication skills. This is also where you may quickly share any professional accomplishments including awards and recognitions that will prompt your audience to want to hear more. A solid Elevator Opening should have the listener wanting to ask questions. You can also mention "transferable skills." Quickly link how you are creative, flexible, resourceful, great with time management, etc.

Strengths

Thirty seconds is not a lot of time so focusing on a core strength is best. If you can slip in two strengths that will be fine. Here are some examples:

- Instead of saying "I have strong communication skills". . . Try "I am a talented motivational speaker and speech writer"
- Instead of saying, "I have a lot computer skills". . . Try "I envisioned our company as a leader in member/client relations so I built a database that allows members and clients to immediately access information usually generated through face-to-face networking sessions. This has saved the company time and money."

Goal(s)

What do you really want? What is your goal? Do you want a job or do you just want exposure to skills that will increase your marketability? Do you want opportunities to network? How can the listener help you to achieve the goal? Here is an example of stating a goal:

- "I am looking for opportunities to develop my management skills within the nonprofit sector."

This statement lets the listener know your specific goal. If the listener has connections with management and nonprofits, he or she will immediately be able to offer guidance. Be specific.

Motivation

The statement or statements you make must reflect the reasons why you are speaking. Your goal and your "ask" are connected to your intrinsic motivators. Most people want to help others as they help themselves. Make sure your statement(s) address your reasons for wanting to share information. Here are some examples:

- "Because I love children, I was hoping to gain more knowledge about childcare and health-related issues at daycare facilities."

- I was inspired when I visited your company and employees shared how they wanted more access to their supervisors. I want to implement sustainable programming to create that pipeline for boosting company-wide morale.

Elevator Opening Examples

1. Hi Dr. Jones. I am a junior Business Administration major at _____ University. My writing is a core skill. I'm interested in securing an entry-level position that will allow me to write and edit documents that minimize complicated jargon. I developed my writing through two internships with XYZ Universal in New York City during my summer breaks. With less time spent trying to understand procedures and more time spent completing procedures, productivity is increased. I want to be a change agent for employer and employee morale.

2. I am an Occupational Safety and Health professional with some training in public relations. I am often sought to give presentations about our company when the vice president is unavailable. They tell me I work well with diverse populations. I'm looking for insight about how I can best position myself for a leadership role in marketing our company. Because I'm inspired by saving lives, I want to help clients and potential clients become better informed about our premier functions that can prevent injuries.

Whether you speak for thirty seconds or two minutes, the Elevator Opening is necessary for effective personal and professional communications.

—Coel

THE INFORMATIVE LECTURE OR KEYNOTE ADDRESS

People are diverse! We all have different experiences. In a class setting, the majority of students want to learn but they also want to get good grades that will help them to get good jobs. In a work environment, the employees and employers want to learn so their earning potential increases. Either way, the listeners at a lecture usually want to understand and retain your message. As a speaker, be ready for outside noise and inner nervousness. Also, you could get horrible nonverbals from the audience members! Be prepared for anything and don't be distracted!

In the following sample outline by high school math teacher Emma L. Millman, there is information about the No Child Left Behind Act. If you were to deliver this speech, your facial expressions should convey enthusiasm about the Act but also disgust for children who are neglected. Your face should reflect your words.

Lecturing About Negative Information

- The introduction should have an uplifting attention grabber

- Introduce the topic without being concrete since the details will follow in the Body of the presentation

- Transition into the reasons why the lecture is not one the audience will be pleased about

- State the issue clearly and be concise

- Try to stay calm so you do not make the sad/bad situation worse

- Try to use supportive language and vocal tonality to soften the impact without appearing you are trying to conceal anything

- The conclusion should be thoughtful and helpful

- If possible, offer information that could shift the focus from negative news to possible solutions

- Sound sincere

As a featured presenter, you should have a strong delivery. Practice having eye contact with all sections of the room while varying your vocal levels, and controlling your planned hand gestures.

Image © Tony Wear, 2009. Used under license from Shutterstock, Inc.

Suggested Aids

Any visual aid that will excite and motivate the audience to listen will be appropriate.
    For the following speech:

- A very large 24 × 28 picture of a child left alone would be good to show how children are left behind

- A dollar bill explaining how more money is needed for education

- A graph of statistics of how education has or has not improved with this Act

A SAMPLE PREPARATION OUTLINE
for
The Informative Lecture or Keynote Address

(Written by Emma L. Millman when she was a secondary education
college student with a mathematics area)

INTRODUCTION

I. Sixty-four percent of the nation's fourth graders cannot solve 2001 minus 25. Yes, sixty-four percent.
(Attention grabber: emotional statements)

II. According to a report by the U.S. Department of Education website accessed December 7, 2013, America's schools are still not producing the math excellence required for global economic leadership and homeland security in the 21st century.
(Introduce the topic and tell why the audience should listen)

III. High school math teachers are still held accountable for teaching students as directed by the No Child Left Behind Act, known as the NCLB. We are all accountable for our children. According to the New York Times website accessed December 7, 2015, this Act was created for every state to set standards in reading and math and for every student to be proficient at those subjects. Students in grades three through eight have been tested yearly and reports have been issued as to whether schools are making "adequate yearly progress" toward that goal.
(Tell why you are qualified to speak)

IV. The NCLB addresses issues such as accountability, teacher quality and incentives for achievement, especially within the area of math.
(Preview the main points)

Transition: The NCLB holds schools accountable for every student's education.

BODY

I. One of the goals of the NCLB is to make sure that schools are teaching what needs to be taught, including the basics like math.

    A. Accountability is measured through yearly testing.

        1. Over the past few years, test scores have been rising slowly. According to the U.S. News website accessed on September 26, 2015, some credit belongs to the NCLB.

        2. An education think tank noted that the NCLB does not deserve full credit since there has been improvement pre-dating it.

    B. Regardless, measurements are in place and math is emphasized in the curriculum.

        1. Former President Bush, once stated that focusing on the basics will improve math education.

        2. However, the NCLB does leave some holes in the math curriculum. By focusing so heavily on what is tested, students are denied a full math education, according to Gordon Cawelti's article in Educational Leadership website accessed May 2, 2015.

        3. In addition, "The National Assessment of Educational Progress" has shown that student achievement grew faster during the years before the No Child Left Behind Act. Scores increased only marginally for eighth graders and not at all for fourth graders, continuing a sluggish trend of slowing achievement growth since the passage of the law. So there are arguments for and against the NCLB.
(First main point with support)

Transition: In order to meet the standards, more qualified teachers are in demand.

    II. The NCLB policy states that highly qualified teachers are required in order to effectively improve education.

        A. These teachers would be the basis for accountability.

            1. In the NCLB's Proven Methods section on September 15, 2004, the government advocated improving and expanding the training of math teachers.

            2. Although some say that this strengthens teachers, some feel it also creates more hoops for them to jump through, according to a student in the Murray State University Education Department in a face-to-face 2014 interview.

        B. In addition to accountability, qualified teachers must also have a strong drive.

            1. The Proven Methods section reflects a teacher's responsibility in a student's education through testing. This is an effective means for teachers to evaluate their teaching.

            2. However, according to Cawelti, a teacher's effectiveness being determined by testing is negatively affecting teacher morale.

        (Second main point with support)

Transition: However, there are incentives offered by the NCLB to help increase teacher morale.

    III. In order to encourage schools to produce positive results, the NCLB offers states and teachers additional funding.

        A. The NCLB offers rewards for states that demonstrate rising achievement.

            1. Schools that make improvements receive more federal grants.

            2. However, if schools do not improve, they risk losing federal funding.

        B. The NCLB also offers monetary rewards for teachers for rising achievements.

            1. Overall, Proven Methods would increase the pay for math and science teachers. But according to the U.S. News website accessed on November 2, 2015, the National Education Association believes that this is unfair to other teachers.

            2. Teachers with students who show exceptional progress are also rewarded with bonuses. However, this is based on test scores alone. This seems unfair to some teachers.

        (Third main point with support)

Connecting words or phrases: The NCLB is a piece of federal legislation designed to improve academics. Some think the legislation is fair; some do not. Its value appears to be subjective.

CONCLUSION

    I. We are in a period of educational reform.

        (Indicate the end)

    II. The NCLB addresses accountability, teacher quality and it offers incentives to promote improvement in academics, with math as one of its main focuses.

        (Summarize your main points)

    III. With measures in place, perhaps one day, all students will be able to solve 2001 minus 25; but in the meantime, as the great mathematical expositor Paul Halmos said, "The only way to learn mathematics is to do mathematics."

        (Creative closures: refer back to the attention grabber and a quotation)

Preparation outline submitted by:
Emma L. Millman, B.A.
High School Math Teacher (Kentucky)

Rough Drafting Your Outline

INTRODUCTION

   I. (Start with a question, quotation, short story, etc.)

   (Attention grabber)

II.

   (Introduce the topic and why you are qualified to speak)

III.

   (Explain the benefits of listening)

IV. Today I will share _____, _____ and _____.

   (Preview the main points)

Transition into the 1st main point:

Body

   I.

      A.

         1.

         2.

      B.

         1.

         2.

      (First main point with supporting material)

Transition into the 2nd main point:

    II.

        A.

        B.

           I.

           2.

        (Second main point with supporting material)

Transition into the 3rd main point:

    III.

        A.

           I.

           2.

        B.

           I.

           2.

CONCLUSION

    I. Thank you for being a great audience.

    (Connect to the audience and indicate the end)

    II.

    (Summary of your main points)
    *REMEMBER: *Your summary of main points should be the same main points introduced in IV. of the preview of the main points from the Introduction*

    III. (End with a quotation, a rhetorical question, a call to act, a refer back to the attention grabber you said in I. of the introduction)

    (Creative Closure)

THE INTRODUCTION OF A KEYNOTE SPEAKER

Either you know this person or you don't. If you know the person, you will only need to confirm important background information. Make sure you don't include personal information that could be embarrassing. It may be funny that you saw him trip over a cat; but that is not appropriate information to share with an audience. Don't make the speaker look or feel silly. If you don't know the speaker, make sure you have the correct pronunciation of the name, company, job title, etc. There is nothing worse than having someone introduce a speaker incorrectly. Giving wrong data about a person will upset most keynote speakers and cause them to lose focus on their presentation. He or she will usually speak out and correct the person introducing him or her. This will cause both parties to be embarrassed and you will look incompetent and unprepared. Your job is to make the speaker sound so interesting that people will be eager to hear what he or she has to say!

Image © 2009 JupiterImages Corporation.

Since this is such a short presentation, you should be very familiar with your presentation and completely engaging! If you are reading off a piece of paper and not having eye contact, you will not create interest for the upcoming speaker. It's your job to make the audience want to listen to the speaker. The introduction can create anticipation or fall flat and force the speaker to create his or her own enthusiasm, thus putting the speaker in a position where he or she has to be great just to counter your lackluster performance.

Suggested Aids

- Show a large picture of the keynote speaker
- Show an object that represents that person's wonderful personality or achievement to stimulate interest in the keynote speaker

---

A SAMPLE PREPARATION OUTLINE
for
The Introduction of a Keynote Speaker

(All references and names are fictitious)

INTRODUCTION

I. Many have seen her but few have heard her words of wisdom.
(Attention grabber: emotional statement)

II. She's here to share her dream for your future. It is a privilege to introduce someone I've known for over ten years.
(Introduce the speaker's topic and tell why you are qualified to introduce the speaker)

III. Her experiences can help all of us learn the benefits of giving back to our communities.
(Explain the benefits of listening)

IV. Her contributions to education and to the well-being of our children are too numerous to mention. From her work with the Big Brother/Big Sister program, to her mission work overseas, she has been the rock that many have leaned upon.
(Preview of the main points: background and/or achievements and future goals and/or reason speaker chose the topic)

Transition: She has been with Big Brothers/Big Sisters for 20 years.

BODY

I. Within this wonderful organization, she has served as a Big Sister, area coordinator and then as the director of one of the largest offices in the United States.

   A. In 2008, it was documented in the August 12th edition of *Best Leaders Magazine* that under her leadership, the membership doubled and the donations tripled. Her vision led to more regional and national participation from celebrities and dignitaries.

   (First main point with support)

Transition: However, her work is not limited to our great country because she has also done mission work overseas.

II. She is selfless. She shares her time and strength with people in smaller countries. As a missionary, she has traveled to Mexico, Africa and even the Middle East helping to build homes, schools and positive relationships.

   A. Tonight, she will show a few slides of her most memorable experiences and allow each one of us to know just how blessed we are to have so many basic needs that we often take for granted.

   (Second main point with support)

CONCLUSION

I. I just don't have the time to tell you how many lives have been enriched through her service.

   (Indicate the end)

II. Her work with Big Brothers and Big Sisters of America and her work as a missionary have expanded her knowledge and her passion for empowering humankind.

   (Summarize your main points)

III. Your keynote presenter is more than a woman of accomplishments; she is a woman of miracles. Please welcome . . . Mrs. Lori . . . Kim . . . Marks!

   (Creative closure: emotional statement)

—*Coel*

Rough Drafting Your Outline

INTRODUCTION

I. (Start with a question, quotation, short story, etc.)

   (Attention grabber)

II. This presenter will share about _____.

   I have known her/him for _____ years.

   (Introduce the topic and why you are qualified to speak)

III.

   (Explain the benefits of listening)

IV.

   (Preview the main points)

   Transition into the 1ˢᵗ main point:

Body

I.

   A.

      1.

      2.

   B.

      1.

      2.

   (First main point with supporting material)

Transition into the 2nd main point:
   II.

       A.

       B.

          1.

          2.

       (Second main point with supporting material)

CONCLUSION
   I.

       (Connect to the audience and indicate the end)

   II.

       (Summary of your main points)
       *REMEMBER: *Your summary of main points should be the same main points introduced in IV. preview of the main points from the Introduction*

   III. I introduce to some & present to all (pause) first name (pause) last name.

       (Creative Closure: emotional statement)

"In a good meeting there is a momentum that comes from the spontaneous exchange of fresh ideas that produces extraordinary results. That momentum depends on the freedom permitted by the participants."

—Harold S. Geneen (1910–97) U.S. telecommunications entrepreneur

From Meaning*less* to Meaning*ful*

The following tips are given by corporate relations expert and doctoral student Elana Kornegay Thompson, M.S.:

In the business world, meetings are inevitable. In many cases after meetings, people walk away asking, "Why did we meet again?" You have the power to take a meeting from meaningless to meaningful. The success or failure of a one-on-one meeting or a strategic planning meeting depends on *preparation, professionalism, participation,* and *pull-through.*

PREPARATION: Preparation is imperative in order to conduct an effective meeting.

- Create and distribute an agenda

- The meeting leader (facilitator) should prepare a clear set of goals, strategies, and points of discussion

- Consider a theme for team meetings to create excitement around the topic

- For example, a meeting that is focused on increasing overall sales could have the theme: ***Drive Up Productivity!***

- A poorly planned meeting that is not executed correctly can lead to additional time-consuming and unproductive meetings

- Make sure all of the appropriate people will be able to attend

- The facilitator should contact all members and make sure the time and location are clear

PROFESSIONALISM

- Arrive on time (early) and show that you value the time of others

- Have set times for beginning and ending the meeting and stick to those times

- Let attendees know up front what will be discussed and what is expected of them

- Switch electronic devices to the "off" position

- Maintain focus and keep discussions on topic

PARTICIPATION

- Appoint a secretary to document key points and action items

- Encourage participation from all attendees. The facilitator must ensure that certain people do not monopolize the conversations

- Ensure that the group stays on topic and does not lack direction and focus

- Only one person should talk at a time

If you are the chairperson for a meeting, you should prepare a Preparation Outline because it's still a presentation.

Image © Andrew Taylor, 2009. Used under license from Shutterstock, Inc.

- Ideas should not be interrupted

- Be brief and concise when speaking

PULL-THROUGH

- Establish clear and defined action steps

- Distribute the meeting minutes

- Distribute action charts with timelines for completion

Elana Kornegay Thompson, ABD
Interim Executive Director
Indianapolis Public School Foundation
Ph.D. Candidate, Indiana State University

This section includes tips and sample outlines from people who have extensive experience with meeting planning and training others to be effective presenters. They explain the different types of meetings that may have some different elements. However, all of the meetings have similar elements from engaging the audience with attention grabbers to distributing agendas and minutes.

You should have no problem with demographics for this presentation. Surveys are easy to do because you don't have to mail them and finding information about your audience is easy because there are numerous people to consult for information.

Many meetings are on-site. Some wonderful employee-centered companies or local organizations offer lunch or comfortable settings for their meetings. The on-site meeting may feel more formal and you will have to adjust your delivery and your message to reach some of the apathetic and cynical audience members who don't want to be there.

Some meetings are held off-site. Off-site meetings are more casual and workers are more receptive to news whether it's good or bad. However, there are usually more distractions when a meeting is held in a public place like a restaurant.

The time of day is crucial for setting a meeting time. Early mornings are probably best with mid-morning meetings as the close second. Meetings after lunch are very non-productive unless activity is involved and even then, most wish to take a nap. The end of the day meeting is the worst as most people will watch the clock and miss or reject most of what you have to say.

If possible, have a team or group activity! Some meetings are so routine and boring if the presenter is not an effective speaker. Use activities and demonstrations to enhance your message, even if it's a negative message. Audiences are receptive to messages that include a visual element. Okay, it's a meeting. Do you really have to practice what you will say? YES! You still need to go over the material you will cover and the presentation aids you will use. You need to make sure your messages are in a proper order with some positive news first, the bad news in the middle and a positive claim at the end. You still need to practice and make sure you don't appear shaky and nervous with constant pacing or hand movement.

Suggested Aids

PowerPoint for staff meetings is good ONLY if pictures and minimal writing are used! There is nothing worse than being subjected to Power-Point presentations early in the morning where the presenter reads blocks of information. BORING! Have pictures and main points with no more than four to five lines of text per slide.

Aids that would be effective at meetings:

- An object like a new coffee mug with the company logo

- An audio or video clip of an organization's television commercial

- A chart with statistics about the team's membership growth

A (BRIEF) SAMPLE PREPARATION OUTLINE
for The Meeting
(ONE-ON-ONE EXISTING CLIENT)

PERSON A: Thanks for joining me today to discuss our plan to increase sales results for Quarter four. I know your time is valuable so let's get started with the items on the agenda . . . We need to discuss Q3 ideas and the budget . . . Tell me, what innovative ideas did you implement in Q3 that you would like to continue for this quarter?

PERSON B: I have reached out to increase customer relations and revenue by increasing face-to-face time with top customers. My team and I have also increased the distribution of marketing items to brand key offices.

PERSON A: What you have done has worked well. How can we achieve even greater success?

PERSON B: I would like to try to do a dinner program with a speaker in an effort to get customers to use more of our products. My team's plan is to target customers that are using more of my competitor's product. We put together these numbers and as you can see if we can win their business we would definitely meet our quarterly goals. A speaker and a banquet would be a nice way to say, "We appreciate you and we want you to make our product your number one choice."

PERSON A: That's good. This brings us to our next item on the agenda, the budget. Where do you stand with your current budget and will it accommodate a program such as this?

PERSON B: I am currently within budget. I have priced the cost of the speaker as well as the dinner cost for 200 attendees. Based on my research I will fully utilize my allocated budget and still have resources available to meet one-on-one with customers.

PERSON A: Should your program exceed your budgeted amount I have additional funds that I could possibly allocate to your team. I would ask that you put together a spreadsheet of the targeted customers for attendance along with their monthly trending. We want to ensure that this dinner makes good business sense and that the appropriate customers are targeted.

PERSON B: I will get that to you by Friday. I believe we have a solid plan in place and that this program would increase sales.

PERSON A: We should follow up in one week to determine if we will move forward with the program. I really like this idea and I feel confident that you and your team can make it happen.

Elana Kornegay Thompson, ABD
Interim Executive Director
Indianapolis Public School Foundation
Ph.D. Candidate, Indiana State University

Strategic Planning Meeting

Turning Ideas into Goals

Director of Communications Jennifer R. Coleman, M.S. offers the following tips for the strategic planning meeting:

- *Adjust the meetings to fit your goals.* Depending on your goals for the strategic planning, it could take hours, days or even years of work! Many organizations strategically plan for the next 20 years!

- *Define your purpose.* Make sure you clearly define your purpose for the meeting so that the group can start to prepare for brainstorming.

- *Review the mission statement.* Make sure that you go over the mission and vision of the organization so that it is remembered during the brainstorming session.

- *Make sure that everyone in the group is engaged.* Remember to ask the group to please turn off their blackberries and cell phones so that there are no distractions during the planning sessions.

Image © Dmitriy Shironosov, 2009. Used under license from Shutterstock, Inc.

- *Do not evaluate during brainstorming.* Before brainstorming, remind the group members that there should be no evaluation of ideas until the brainstorming session is over. The purpose of brainstorming is to generate ideas, not discuss them. Discussion can take place after brainstorming, or during the next meeting.

- *Don't be afraid of silence.* It may take time for the group to loosen up and really start offering ideas. Facilitate by asking questions; but allow some silence for people to answer. If you keep talking, they are unlikely to interrupt you with their ideas.

- *Don't let the group go off topic.* During group discussions and brainstorming, it is very easy for a group to go off topic. This can happen very quickly. If you feel the meeting is going off topic, remember to bring the group members back to the main focus by reviewing the specific purpose of the meeting, while still acknowledging that the ideas are good.

- *Find a volunteer recorder/secretary.* Pick a volunteer before the meeting begins to be your "recorder/secretary." You can use a large flip chart, marker board or even PowerPoint for your volunteer to write down the group's ideas as the brainstorming is taking place. Use whatever is the most convenient for your situation. Make sure that your audience can see what is being written. Flip charts are probably more suited for smaller groups, whereas PowerPoint on a large projector screen is better for larger groups in larger rooms.

- *Be positive and enthusiastic!* Strategic planning is a creative meeting that is meant to generate ideas. Be positive about the ideas given during brainstorming and enthusiastic about the planning process. If you look bored, your audience will be bored too!

Jennifer R. Coleman, M.S.
Director of Communications
Ohio Soybean Council

A SAMPLE PREPARATION OUTLINE
for The Meeting
(STRATEGIC PLANNING)

INTRODUCTION

I. A man by the name of Terence Cooke once said, "America's greatness is not only recorded in books, but it is also dependent upon each and every citizen being able to utilize public libraries."
   (Attention grabber: quotation)

II. As you are all aware, community involvement in the City Library has decreased significantly over the past three years. I called this meeting of the entire City Library Board of Directors because I have been an active member of this board for over 10 years now and I have seen downward trends of interest in the library.
(Introduce the topic and tell why you are qualified to speak)

III. We all serve on the library board because we all believe in the benefits a public library can offer to a community, but in order to keep it open for the next generations, we must find new ways to bring people back to the library.
(Explain the benefits of listening)

IV. While we have many challenges ahead, the main issues we need to discuss today are the decreasing use of the community meeting rooms, the decrease in books being checked out from the library and the things we could do to increase the library's popularity in the community.
(Preview the main points)

Transition: The upstairs meeting rooms have been an important part of this library for many years.

BODY

I. Since it was built in 1982, local businesses, government officials and schools have used the library regularly as a meeting location for a variety of activities.
   A. But according to our research, the use of the upstairs meeting rooms has decreased by 65% over the last three years! That is a big drop ladies and gentlemen.
   B. We've seen some major competition from the new hotel that was built just down the road. This hotel offers the same central location as the library, but has catering services and newly decorated meeting rooms. The hotel charges a fee for the use of its meeting rooms, and the library does not; however, the hotel's prices are not unreasonable.
   (First main point with support)

Transition: But the usage of the library meeting rooms is not the only library service that is struggling.

II. I think that we would all agree that checking out books is the main purpose of a library and the most significant benefit it can offer a community. The fact that this number is decreasing is a major concern.
   A. The research shows a 50% decrease in the number of books that are being checked out compared to three years ago.
   B. We believe that this decrease comes from the rising popularity of online bookstores. People seem to be more willing to pay for their books online, rather than take the time to visit the library and check them out.
   (Second main point with support)

Transition: Now that we've reviewed the situation, it's time to start planning for the future of the City Library.

III. While we are brainstorming, it is important to remember that the mission of the City Library is to provide free access to knowledge and to serve as a community center for educational activities. I'd like to hear your ideas for increasing the library's popularity.
   A. Brainstorming Session I (Community Meeting Rooms)
   B. Brainstorming Session II (Book Checkout)
   (Third main point with support)

CONCLUSION

I. It was a little difficult at times today, but this has been a great meeting.
   (Indicate the end)

II. We've looked at the decreasing use of the community meeting rooms, the decrease in books being checked out from the library; and we developed ideas for what we could do to increase the library's popularity in the community.
(Summarize your main points)

III. We still have a long way to go to bring the popularity of the City Library back to what it used to be, and we'll have many more meetings like this one to accomplish that goal. But I know we all believe in the public library system and what it brings to the community. I do not intend to give up this fight, because public libraries are a part of America's greatness.
(Creative closures: emotional statements and a refer back to the attention grabber)

Tips and preparation outline submitted by:
Jennifer R. Coleman, M.S.
Director of Communications
Ohio Soybean Council

Basic Report of Information Meeting

A SAMPLE PREPARATION OUTLINE
for
The Meeting
(BASIC REPORT OF INFORMATION)

INTRODUCTION

I. So why are we here?
(Attention grabber: rhetorical question)

II. Everyone has been whispering and the rumors are extensive; but today, you'll learn why we needed to change our vacation policy. I was asked to speak because I've been in the budget office for over two years now and I've seen the financial crisis this company has been going through.
(Introduce the topic and tell why you are qualified to speak)

III. This policy change affects all of us in this room but if we understand the changes we will be able to adjust our vacation dates, our family budgets and our personal time.
(Explain the benefits of listening)

IV. There are two main things that have changed: personal days have been cut from three days to two days and you will no longer be able to get your vacation money early.
(Preview the main points)

Transition: I know you are probably disgusted, but we can only have two personal days now.

BODY

I. Personal days have always been appreciated. I know that I have needed those days for family outings, doctor's appointments and plain old rest!
   A. Unfortunately, when people are away, we don't produce as much. This year, due to the war and other situations, we don't have as many clients. However, the work is still steady even though it hasn't been as great as previous years.
   B. With people out, it takes longer to finish our products and it puts us behind. Right now, we could not afford to take more clients if we wanted them because our manpower is too low. Therefore, we cannot afford to have too many people out at the same time and due to finances, we cannot afford to pay for more than two paid personal days. I am so very sorry but it affects me too.
   (First main point with support)

Transition: Of course, the "good news" continues with the reason why we can't get the vacation money early.

II. In the past, all of us could get our vacation money so we could have more money when we went away. Unfortunately, we can no longer expect this to happen.

    A. Once you get your paycheck on Friday, you will not be able to get your next check until the following Friday.

        1. This is a hardship for those who looked forward to that extra money for the family trip; however, you can always go to the company Credit Union and borrow the extra money and pay it back if you need money badly.

        2. This is an option. It's not a great option; but it's an option nonetheless.

    B. The Credit Union will be very flexible with the loans since the new policies are taking effect. The loan officers will help as much as they can.

        1. The Union is open Monday through Friday from 9 A.M. until 5 P.M.

        2. Please use this resource if you need extra funds.

    (Second main point with support)

CONCLUSION

I. It hasn't been pleasant but at least you now know why things have changed.
(Indicate the end)

II. So yes, it's from three days to two days and advances won't be allowed. It hurts and it affects all of us.
(Summarize your main points)

III. But you know what? We are all here so we can earn a living for ourselves and our families and even though these are bad times, perhaps we should find something positive about this and keep our spirits alive. As someone once said, "What doesn't kill us, makes us stronger."
(Creative closures: question, emotional statements, and a quotation)

—Coel

Rough Drafting Your Outline

INTRODUCTION

I. (Start with a question, quotation, short story, etc.)

  (Attention grabber)

II.

  (Introduce the topic and why you are qualified to speak)

III. These topics reflect the changes we all could face this year including pay cuts!

  (Explain the benefits of listening)

IV.

  (Preview the main points)

  Transition into the 1st main point:

Body

I.

  A.

   1.

   2.

  B.

   1.

   2.

  (First main point with supporting material)

Transition into the 2nd main point:

   II.

       A.

       B.

         1.

         2.

       (Second main point with supporting material)

Transition into the 3rd main point:

   III.

       A.

         1.

         2.

       B.

         1.

         2.

CONCLUSION

   I. Thanks for listening during this difficult time at our company.

       (Connect to the audience and indicate the end)

   II.

       (Summary of your main points)
       REMEMBER: *Your summary of main points should be the same main points introduced in IV. preview of the main points from the Introduction*

   III. (End with a quotation, a rhetorical question, a call to act, a refer back to the attention grabber you said in I. of the introduction)

       (Creative Closure)

The Past, Present and Future Self-Introduction
Sample Outline

INTRODUCTION

I. Don't you like meeting new people?
   (Attention grabber: rhetorical question)

II. I do! But I also want you to learn a little about me. No one on earth knows me better than little old me.
   (Introduce the topic and why you are qualified to speak)

III. We grow when we open our minds and listen to new people. We do not have to agree with a person's lifestyle or the message, to listen with kindness and respect.
   (Explain the benefits of listening)

IV. Today, I will share a glimpse of who I was, who I am and who I hope to be.
   (Preview the main points)

Transition: My past is filled with both pain and joy.

Body

I. I once was self-absorbed and this lead to obsessions that brought hurt & happiness.
   A. I was obsessed with being popular.
      1. I remember hurting people by saying something mean or by inaction.
      2. A teacher yelled at me in high school because a friend cried. I felt so bad because I did not defend her and I allowed her to be the victim of someone who was more self-absorbed than I was. I felt her pain.
   B. The realization of my own weaknesses allowed me to want more from life so I became obsessed with joy.
      1. I started to do random acts of kindness.
         a. I would pay for the person behind me in the drive-thru line at a fast food place, over-tip a server, babysit for free and the list goes on.
      2. I learned that status meant nothing; and I found that joy did not come from what I had but who I wanted to be.
   (First main point and support)

Transition: My past is a little part of who I am today.

II. I am a work in progress.
   A. My career has been progressive.
      1. I have gone from basic company duties to expanded responsibilities.
      2. I chair committees and I lead several teams in the workplace.
   B. My personal life has been progressive.
      1. I have made new friends, re-evaluated some old friends and watched my love shift over the years.
      2. Things I once thought were important are not as important today.
      3. Love, faith and strength are connected and wanting loved ones safe and healthy seem to top the list now. It is my want and my need to help others as I grow stronger.
   (Second main point and support)

Internal Summary: You know a little about my past and my present; and my future is full of opportunities.

III. I have the opportunity to graduate and attend graduate school.
   A. Malcolm X said "the future belong to those who prepare for it today."
      1. I have met with my academic adviser and created a list of graduate programs.
      2. I plan to apply to two programs that would be my absolute dream programs.

3. I will send applications to three realistic programs and then at least one I am sure will accept my credentials.

4. I have already made appointments with our Career Services Office so I can polish my interview skills and writing skills. I want my application process to be organized and outstanding.

B. The opportunity to work in the family business is also an opportunity that could serve me well.

1. I know everything about our business. I have been training since I was six years old.

2. My favorite part of the business is watching our customers go home satisfied. That brings me joy and I want joy in my future.

(Third main point and support)

CONCLUSION

I. I am amazed at how much I have really grown over the years.
(Indicate the end)

II. Today, I have shared my past, my present and dreams for my future.
(Summarize your main points)

III. I have an open mind and I DO like to listen to new people; so if you can share a glimpse of who <u>you</u> are, that would bring me joy and help me to be all I hope to be.
(Creative closure: emotional statement)

—Coel

Rough Drafting Your Outline

INTRODUCTION

  I. (Start with a direct or rhetorical question, a quotation, a short story, etc.)

    (Attention grabber)

II.

    (Introduce the topic and why you are qualified to speak)

III.

    (Explain the benefits of listening)

IV.

    (Preview the main points)

    Transition into the 1st main point:

Body

  I.

    A.

      1.

      2.

    B.

      1.

      2.

    (First main point with supporting material)

Transition into the 2nd main point:
    II.

        A.

        B.

            I.

            2.

        (Second main point with supporting material)

Transition into the 3rd main point:
    III.

        A.

            I.

            2.

        B.

            I.

            2.

CONCLUSION
    I.

        (Connect to the audience and indicate the end)

    II.

        (Summary of your main points)
        *REMEMBER: *Your summary of main points should be the same main points introduced in IV. preview of the main points from the Introduction*

    III. (End with a quotation, a rhetorical question, a call to act, a refer back to the attention grabber you said in I. of the introduction)

    (Creative Closure)

People want to be inspired and motivated to be the best they can be. From the commencement to the annual conference, people have been waiting all year for that special speech from that special person. You are that person! You were asked to be the main event so you have to bring it! It doesn't matter what the demographics are. The attitudes and values will vary. Your job is to make people feel empowered and moved to change and improve themselves and others.

Image © 2009 JupiterImages Corporation.

A persuasive keynote address may be right after a meal and part of a banquet. It could be late in the morning and right before lunch. It could be at any time BUT it is rare for a keynote address to be before 10 A.M. It's usually around lunch or dinner/supper or as a late night opening ceremony speech for a weekend conference.

Microphones are a must! Wear a lavaliere microphone even if you have a podium/lectern because this way you can walk around. A keynote should involve some animated movement so that emotional levels are high. Make sure you are loud, articulate and expressive. Your delivery outline should be typed and placed into a conservative portfolio that compliments your attire; but you can never go wrong with basic black. Memorize the introduction and conclusion. Know your presentation well enough to lose your place and yet know where you are in your presentation.

Suggested Aids

- PowerPoint slides of pictures or data can be effective but MINIMAL use is encouraged.

- Handouts are not great if the audience is large. Paper can be noisy so any information that can be put on a slide or the use of a large object would be best. Let your words and the way you say them be the focus of a keynote address. Vivid language and a strong delivery will surpass the effectiveness of aids any day. Most famous speakers are remembered for speeches that had few if any presentation aids.

Former President Obama is giving a persuasive keynote address.

Image © Terry Underwood Evans, 2009. Used underlicense from Shutterstock, Inc.

Problem-Solution or Cause-Effect Formats

Presenting problems and solutions or stating causes and effects are persuasive messages often used to move audiences to consider change. The outlines for these messages are quite similar. The following is a sample preparation outline for a presentation that identifies problems and potential solutions. Notice the main points within the body of the outline. The problems and solutions could easily be substituted with the causes and effects. This outline is structured to fit both types of persuasive presentations.

A SAMPLE PREPARATION OUTLINE
for
The Persuasive Keynote Address
(PROBLEM-SOLUTION FORMAT)

(For people who embrace positive changes)

INTRODUCTION

  I. We have problems . . . in our country . . . in our homes . . . in our souls.
    (Attention grabber: emotional statements)

  II. We have problems in our country when our children know more about birth control than financial planning. We have problems in our homes when we care more about what the neighbors think about us than what our children think about us. We have problems in our souls when we preach the things we never practice because it's easier to point fingers outward rather than point fingers inward. We have problems; but I'm not talking to anyone in this room, right?

     I'm talking about those *other* people.

     Now, of course, who am I to even say these things? I'm just a stranger. You know, the director of some organization who was invited to speak to you today because they needed a speaker.
    (Introduce the subject and tell why you are qualified to speak)

  III. The things I say are not things that really apply to you personally. So, just ignore whatever isn't applicable to you. I certainly wouldn't want to offend anyone . . . actually make anyone look deep inside to see if he or she is part of the problem . . . I wouldn't do that. Why would self-reflection change the country, the home, the soul?
    (Explain the benefits of listening)

  IV. So for those other people . . . let's look at two problems before exploring two solutions.
    (Preview the main points)

Transition: In America, two-parent homes are declining.

BODY

  I. There are two key problems.
    A. First, a broken home is often associated with divorce and an absent mother or father.
      1. But broken often reflects a broken spirit and a loss of hope.
        a. According to the CNN Politics website accessed January 31, 2012, 85 percent of Americans had hope in 1999. In 2012, only 58 percent felt optimistic.
      2. When you lose hope, you lose the "will" to get better. When you lose hope, YOU are broken.
        a. You sit and do nothing, say nothing, and feel nothing.
      3. Broken is that inability to see anything but the negative aspects of our circumstances.
        a. A broken spirit creates a broken home that affects all of us . . . eventually.
        (First main point with support)

Transition: Of course, some people, no one here, but some suffer from broken promises.

    B. Despite good intentions, promises are made knowing that they really can not be kept.
      1. We promise our children things we can not financially afford.
        a. We want them to love us so we tell them they can have another material object because we are way too busy to actually share our time with them.
        b. We work two jobs and we are exhausted.

2. We promise our co-workers things we really don't have time to do.
    a. But we want that promotion. We need that validation so that we can feel good about ourselves when things at home are falling apart.
    b. After all, at least we "look good" at the office.
3. We hear promises from our leaders.
    a. We hear promises about new programs and new research.
    b. But they forget to tell us that these promises are impossible to implement without other factors taking place like funding, a majority vote or an organized plan.
    (First main point with support)

Transitions: We suffer from broken homes and broken promises; but are there any solutions?

II. Sure, the solutions are simple.
    A. Honesty is the first step towards changing the outside or the inside.
        1. People say they are honest and yet I see beautiful cars driven by sad faces.
            a. I recently conducted a survey at a local mall . . . in an area of the city that is perceived to be affluent.
            b. One out of four adults said they were content but not really happy.
            c. They said that they wished their families were more strong and loving.
        2. People say they are honest and yet I see gifts wrapped in beautiful tissue paper and opened by those who drink to dull the pain.
            a. They smoke to ease nervousness.
            b. They take pills to cover the depression.
            c. Those *other* people say they are honest and yet I also see designer logos on purses, luggage and shirts owned by people who cry "Why don't they really love me and have time for me?"

Transitions: Getting honest means you know that at some point you may have been one of the **other** people; with honesty, people have the desire to change . . . to get active.

    B. Getting active, is the other solution.
        1. It doesn't take more money or more effort, to spend more time with your family.
            a. It only takes more wisdom. Turn off the gadgets, put down the paper, and talk to your loved ones.
            b. That's all they want and that's most of what they need.
        2. Mr. Edwards was a well-intentioned father. He worked ten hour shifts each day to provide for his three children and for his wife.
            a. When his oldest daughter started acting funny, he ignored the signs. He ignored her quiet demeanor. He ignored her change in clothing styles. He ignored her new friends.
            b. He was busy. He was tired. He was making money. It wasn't until after she got shot, that the bullet pierced his soul.
            c. He had forgotten how to be a father in the most basic sense. He forgot how to hug his family when he came home. He forgot how to mandate family dinners instead of allowing his kids to eat whatever, whenever, and with whomever. But once his daughter was almost killed, he changed.
            d. He got active in the lives of all of his children . . . and it did not take more money . . . it took more wisdom.
    (Second main point with support)

CONCLUSION

I. Why is this the keynote address for your corporation? Why am I not talking about products or numbers or employee rights? It's simple . . . because what you bring to work with you—will ultimately determine what happens to you . . . at XYZ Corporation.
    (Indicate the end)

II. Get honest so that you have the desire and energy to get active. Take care of your country by minimizing your potential to be one of the other people. Take care of your homes so that when you come to work you feel energized and not victimized. Take care of your soul . . . don't sell that. Take care of your soul and keep your mind focused on important things and not on superficial things.
(Summarize your main points)

III. Sure, we have problems. But with honesty and activism, those problems can just be hurdles for all of us to jump over on our way to the finish line, where we all win! Whether you are an XYZ employee, loved one or stranger like me, it's a team effort. All of us can win this time. We can have a healthy country, a healthy home and a healthy soul. It starts with us. Embrace your God-given greatness. Reject the fear and what I call that demonic spirit of laziness and averageness. Today, join me and make the proclamation: Mediocrity is not an option! Thank you for inviting me to share a message. Have a successful year! Remember . . . Get honest. Get active. Get ready!
(Creative closure: emotional statements)

—Coel

Persuasion does involve selling yourself & your ideas. However, just the word "sales" will cause some people to become uncomfortable. Therefore, assuring people that you won't pressure them or make them feel guilty, serve in your favor. Explain the main points of your message, the benefits attained from listening, then be knowledgeable and sincere. Those things will work more than high pressure sales tactics.

A seasoned employee benefits expert wrote the following tips. Lori Starkman Shapiro received her Bachelor of Science in Mathematics from the University of Delaware. She is currently a Senior Vice President at Fidelity Investments in Suburban Philadelphia, PA. Her knowledge of ethical sales practices is outstanding. With over twenty-five years of expertise, sales training and award-winning results, she is more than qualified to offer the following:

Sell, Sell, Sell!

Please Do Your Homework—Know your audience; research the people/person you are selling to; try to make a connection; take a few minutes to check your target's Website or social media pages—not only will they show that you did your homework, it will make your audience feel good.

Phone a Friend—Determine if there is anyone you know. Ask for guidance and insight about your target audience. Don't be afraid to ask; you'll be surprised how willing others are to help.

Know Your Buyer (Audience)—While you don't want to ignore the others who might be included in the process, it's important to know who has the power to ultimately make the decision.

Have a Plan—Know what you are going to say and when—timing counts. Be sure not to leave the room or to hang up the phone without having covered the features, advantages and benefits of your product/service; always have a contingency plan if you are cut short.

Rough Drafting Your Problem-Solution
or Cause-Effect Outline

INTRODUCTION

I. (Start with a question, quotation, short story, etc.)

(Attention grabber)

II.

(Introduce the topic and why you are qualified to speak)

III.

(Explain the benefits of listening)

IV.

(Preview the main points)

Transition into the 1st main point:

Body

I. The first main point is all about the . . . . .

   A.

      1.

      2.

   B.

      1.

      2.

(First main point with supporting material)

Transition into the 2nd main point:

   II.

        A.

        B.

           1.

           2.

        (Second main point with supporting material)

CONCLUSION

   I.

        (Connect to the audience and indicate the end)

   II.

        (Summary of your main points)
        *REMEMBER: *Your summary of main points should be the same main points introduced in IV. preview of the main points from the Introduction*

   III. (End with a quotation, a rhetorical question, a call to act, a refer back to the attention grabber you said in I. of the introduction)

        (Creative Closure)

Rough Drafting Monroe's
Motivated Sequence

Step 1—ATTENTION

(Start with a question, quotation, short story, etc. Some people include a preview of the main points & some do not.)

Step 2—NEED

This step shows how the topic links to the psychological need of the audience. Explain that there is a huge problem that needs a solution. This step is all about the problem. Do not tell us to do anything during this step. Build your case with research showing there are issues. For example, if you want us to donate to homeless shelters, do not discuss donating in the Need step. Tell us about how many homeless people there are in the Unites States. Discuss the horrible circumstances people face.

Step 3—SATISFACTION

This is the step where you present the solution(s). You also support your solution(s) with research that proves your solution(s) will work. Here is where you tell us that donating money will help solve the homeless problem.

Step 4—VISUALIZATION

So we can visualize all you have shared, tell us the great things that will happen if we listen to you. Then tell us the bad result if we do not listen to you.

Step 5—ACTION

Call people to do something or to believe something. Often, starting with the word "please" is a good opening word for the call to act.

THE PET PEEVE RELEASE EXERCISE

This is often a **first** presentation because there are varying degrees of nervousness and tension. As a result, people may approach the podium fearful. They may want to speak softly or read the entire speech, instead of giving prolonged eye contact. Therefore, this fun speech is "organized venting." It is a structured presentation; but you get to complain, which helps to minimize the fear.

Reflect on how you feel. You may want to sway back and forth or clear your throat or let your hands and fingers pop up and down off the podium. Such behavior is probably caused by thinking of yourself and how you are doing, instead of concentrating on delivering an important message to your audience.

One way to overcome tension and nervousness is to talk about something that really creates energy within you. This presentation is designed to give you a fun speaking experience for which you cast aside all inhibitions, fears, and thoughts of yourself. See what you can do with it.

Explanation

This is an *informative lecture*. You will inform us about your pet peeve. It should concern your innermost feelings, which arouse in you a great disturbance and feeling of anger, more than anything else. It should make your blood boil just to think of it. Your presentation may be about a person, place or thing. The topic should be relevant today so that you get disturbed thinking about it right now! Smiles. Most students speak about slow drivers and dirty roommates.

How To Prepare

First, decide what your most annoying and irritating pet peeve is. Secondly, come up with 2-4 main points. These can be reasons why this person, place or thing bothers you so much. Thirdly, use "support" by giving an example, fact, testimony, etc. that explains each main point or reason. Finally, put your thoughts into a PREPARATION OUTLINE format and rehearse. After rehearsing, condense your outline into a Delivery Outline for use on the day you give this lecture.

How To Deliver Your Presentation

There is just one way to deliver a speech about a pet peeve. Put your whole body and soul into it. Mean every word. Use plenty of force and vivid (but tasteful) language. Let a slow fire that has been smoldering within you suddenly blaze up but with an organized structure and with purposeful gestures. If your arms feel like waving, let them wave. (But don't let them wave constantly!—You still need to be professional and controlled). If you feel like shouting, then shout. You will be surprised at your own ability—when you really "unload" your pet peeve.

A SAMPLE PREPARATION OUTLINE
for
The Pet Peeve Release

INTRODUCTION

I. Does lying bother you?
   (Attention grabber: rhetorical question)

II. Lying bothers me a lot.
   (Introduce the topic and why you are qualified to speak)

III. By sharing, I want you to know you are not alone if you too have been a victim.
(Explain the benefits of listening)

IV. Lying affects my ability to focus on my work and my ability to trust others.
(Preview the main points)

Transition: I have trouble focusing at work once I feel betrayed.

BODY

I. My whole day was affected by a recent lie I was told.
  A. My day started well but the lie shifted my focus.
   1. A friend told me that she was using the money I had given her for bills. Instead of using it to pay her bills, she went on a vacation to the Bahamas with some friends
  B. Dealing with outside and internal challenges can be emotionally draining.
   1. Trying to make it through the day after being lied to is difficult but not impossible. It requires a lot of energy and I often surround myself with positive speaking people.
   2. Knowing that I lost money and a friend made me watch the clock and hope for the day to be over.
   (First main point with support)

Transition: My work day is not the only thing that is affected; my ability to trust also diminishes.

II. Losing trust is not good.
  A. I can forgive a person.
   1. However, I may not wish to be a lifelong friend anymore. I do believe it is important to forgive; but it is also important to protect oneself from people and things that can cause physical or emotional harm.
   2. A lack of trust could hinder one from reaching out to someone who could be a blessing to his or her life.
  B. Building trust is not impossible; but it takes time. I am certainly not going to be quick in sharing my feelings or my finances!
   1. I still have many friends. I share pain and laughter. I still nurture friendships through giving and through some trust.
   2. However, to minimize the potential for harming the relationship, I let friends know my limits. I will give my friends money. I don't loan them money. There is no expectation when I present a gift.
   (Second main point with support)

CONCLUSION

I. Being lied to causes negative perceptions.
(Indicate the end)

II. It affects my ability to focus on my work and my ability to trust others.
(Summarize your main points)

III. But the question is . . . are YOU honest?
(Creative closure: rhetorical question)

—Coel

Rough Drafting Your Outline

INTRODUCTION

  I. (Start with a question, quotation, short story, etc.)

    (Attention grabber)

II.

    (Introduce the topic and why you are qualified to speak)

III.

    (Explain the benefits of listening)

IV.

    (Preview the main points)

Transition into the 1st main point:

Body

  I.

    A.

      1.

      2.

    B.

      1.

      2.

    (First main point with supporting material)

Transition into the 2nd main point:

    II.

        A.

        B.

            I.

            2.

        (Second main point with supporting material)

Transition into the 3rd main point:

    III.

        A.

            I.

            2.

        B.

            I.

            2.

CONCLUSION

    I.

        (Connect to the audience and indicate the end)

    II.

        (Summary of your main points)
        *REMEMBER: *Your summary of main points should be the same main points introduced in IV. preview of the main points from the Introduction*

    III. (End with a quotation, a rhetorical question, a call to act, a refer back to the attention grabber you said in I. of the introduction)

        (Creative Closure)

THE PRESENTATION OF AN AWARD OR GIFT

You have the pleasure of presenting an honor to someone who deserves it. You need to be genuine, well-rehearsed, poised and enthusiastic! If you have a bland performance, you will dishonor the recipient. Just like introducing a speaker, it's your job to build excitement for this individual and for the audience.

Make sure you either know the recipient, have the opportunity to speak to the recipient, or have the chance to check all the information you are about to say about the recipient. You need to make sure you have his or her name correct. Make sure the accomplishments you are about to state, are correct. Make sure the information is tasteful and complete. Practice this presentation.

Dr. Karen Hill Johnson shares her example of a speech of presentation.

Suggested Aids

This very short speech does not need an aid other than the object you are presenting.

Image © Ilin Sergey, 2009. Used under license from Shutterstock, Inc.

A SAMPLE PREPARATION OUTLINE
for
The Presentation of an Award or Gift

INTRODUCTION

I. "I call it like I see it," "On your feet," "Just keeping it real."
   (Attention grabber: quotations)

II. These quotes are just a few we hear from this professor in the Speech Communication Department at West Eastern University.
   (Introduce the topic)

III. The students have voted and this year, the vote was unanimous. I am proud to say I was one of the students who voted for this wonderful professor who touched my life two years ago when I was in her class.
   (Tell why you are qualified to speak)

IV. Today, you will know the reasons why students chose this educator for the distinguished "Profound Professor Award" before I tell you about the recipient.
   (Preview the main points)

Signpost: First, let's hear the reasons why the students voted for this profound professor.

BODY

I. When submitting nominations for this award, students supported their votes with the following comments:
   A. "This professor actually made me work for my A."
   B. "She called me out when I was slacking and because of that, I really applied myself for the first time as a student."

    C. "She set me up for success with encouraging words and realistic objectives."

    D. "Through tough-love, she showed me how to be the best I could be."

    (First main point with support)

Transition: Now that we know why the students voted for this professor, let's find out more about who she is.

  II. This professor can be seen in her office outside of scheduled office hours coaching students on their persuasive speeches, buying stock-piles of red ink pens for grading, driving the 15-passenger van to speech competitions.

    A. She motivates students through her honest dialogue and pushes us to reach our ultimate potential.

    B. This professor goes above and beyond to influence students in a positive way even if we hate it at first! She calls us. She emails us. She shows up at our houses when we pretend to be sick. It's intimidating but also refreshing.

    (Second main point with support)

CONCLUSION

  I. There's so much I could say but I promised I would be brief.

  (Indicate the end)

  II. There are so many reasons she is deserving of this honor and I am proud to be the one to present it to such a worthy person.

  (Summarize your main points)

  III. Because this professor goes above and beyond the standard of excellence through her dedication and sincere concern for students, this year's Profound Professor Award goes to Dr. Chris Wilson Hall.

  (Creative closure: emotional statement)

Preparation outline submitted by:
Karen Hill Johnson, Ed.D.
Instructor of Communications
West Kentucky Community and Technical College
Freelance Communication Consultant

Rough Drafting Your Outline

INTRODUCTION

I. (Start with a question, quotation, short story, etc.)

   (Attention grabber)

II.

   (Introduce the topic and why you are qualified to speak)

III.

   (Explain the benefits of listening)

IV.

   (Preview the main points)

   Transition into the 1st main point:

Body

I.

   A.

      1.

      2.

   B.

      1.

      2.

   (First main point with supporting material)

Transition into the 2nd main point:
II.

    A.

    B.

      1.

      2.

    (Second main point with supporting material)

Transition into the 3rd main point:
III.

    A.

      1.

      2.

    B.

      1.

      2.

CONCLUSION
  I.

    (Connect to the audience and indicate the end)

  II.

    (Summary of your main points)
    *REMEMBER: *Your summary of main points should be the same main points introduced in IV. preview of the main points from the Introduction*

  III. (End with a quotation, a rhetorical question, a call to act or a refer back to the attention grabber you said in I. of the introduction)

    (Creative Closure)

PRESENTING WITH A TEAM

Understanding the TEAM Introduction and Conclusion Given by the Moderator/Facilitator

When you conduct a TEAM presentation, the team should appoint a moderator or facilitator. Even if you wish to introduce each other one by one and present equal sections of material, someone needs to open and close the forum and the entire presentation. You do not want to appear unorganized.

The four elements of an Introduction and the three elements of a Conclusion are still necessary. However, there are some slight modifications for teams. Here are the general elements of a TEAM INTRODUCTION given by the moderator or facilitator:

- Attention Grabber
- Introduce the team/organization's name, the topic and the moderator's or facilitator's name
- Give the benefits for listening
- Introduce the team members and their subtopics

The TEAM CONCLUSION given by the moderator or facilitator includes:

- Indicating the end and thanking the audience for listening on behalf of your team/organization
- Summarizing the main points
- Having the "Creative Closure"
- A forum if required or requested
- A SECOND Closure if there is a forum

Creating the Transitions Between Each Presenter

Make sure there is some type of transition between presenters. The moderator or facilitator can keep introducing the presenters or the team members can one-by-one introduce the next speaker. It does not matter as long as there are smooth transitions:

Moderator or Facilitator: Your next speaker will share insight about European travel.

Team Member: Bob will now share insight about European travel.

THE MODERATING OR FACILITATING OF AN *EVENT*

Most people want to be at an event that requires moderating/facilitating. Regardless of the formality, people want to feel appreciated for attending. If the audience is made up of children, adults, or both, the moderator/facilitator or Master or Mistress of ceremonies sets the tone for the entire event. If you don't make people feel happy to be there, they won't get the maximum joy for attending that event. You must be organized and energetic for the crowd to respond favorably before, during and after the event.

Most formal or informal events are in the late afternoon or evening. Flashy attire can work for this type of presentation because you are the first and last person the audience will see. Exciting attire will actually excite the audience and make people aware of the magnitude of the event. "Flashy and exciting" do not mean tacky. Too much flesh showing or too many wardrobe distractions can take away from the keynote speaker or activities. You want to enhance the event with your presence not serve as a solo act.

The Moderator or Facilitator

The terms "moderator" and "facilitator" are very similar. They both represent a person responsible for keeping an event organized and running smoothly. Usually a "moderator" is associated with a debate, roast, panel discussion or team symposium where introductions are needed and forums are probable. A "facilitator" is associated with workshops/seminars that involve a lot of audience interaction. Both terms are used interchangeably and that is fine. However, keep in mind that the moderator is usually JUST a host who is expected to keep the event or presentation organized and on time. He/she is also expected to limit his/her comments. A facilitator is more of an educator and host combined.

Events that are memorable, often have outstanding moderators. Most effective seminars and workshops have trained facilitators. The moderator and facilitator are supposed to be articulate, organized, motivated and motivating. A good moderator/ facilitator pays attention to time constraints and audience feedback. If you have been asked to play one of these important roles, you must be ready for anything. You may need to add an activity or delete a sub-topic based on audience interactions or interruptions. A great moderator/ facilitator does not lose his or her composure no matter what happens. Losing your composure will not only affect your credibility as a professional but it will make the audience uncomfortable! You must be ready for any external or internal noise. Even if you become ill in front of an audience, you need to quickly close the session with poise and professionalism. If you are going to be a moderator/facilitator:

- Have a creative attention grabber. Don't just say, "Hi, welcome to this event." Grab the audience's attention and be creative and exciting!

- Introduce the name of your team/organization; then introduce yourself and any other moderators/facilitators unless you and the other moderators/facilitators are introduced

- Introduce the topic or state the event theme; and introduce any participants you need to introduce

- Introduce all team members, their titles and sub-topic areas if applicable

- If needed, have presentation aids that add clarity and vividness to the message

- Guide the session and make sure there is no "dead air." Always be ready to ask a question or start an activity

- At the end of the event, but BEFORE the creative closure, thank the participants/audience members

- Summarize the main points

The master/mistress of ceremonies should display enthusiasm so that people will be glad they came to the event.

Image © Julia Enterprises, 2009. Used under license from Shutterstock, Inc.

- End with a creative closure to make the session memorable

- If there is a forum of questions and answers, make sure you have a SECOND creative closure! NEVER end with, "Well, I guess that's it. Thank you for coming." That is a horrible way to end!

THE TEAM SYMPOSIUM (WITH A MODERATOR)

The Team Symposium is similar to the Panel Discussion. Both are team presentations. They both have moderators who introduce the topic, the sub-topics and the presenters. The Panel Discussion is an interactive continuous forum of comments, questions and answers given by the moderator, panelists and audience members. Therefore,the three part conclusion comes AFTER the "forum." There is no need for a second closure.The Team Symposium has a conclusion, a forum and a SECOND closure.

The primary difference between the symposium and the panel discussion is that a symposium requires short prepared speeches and a panel discussion is a discussion with back and forth dialogue and feedback. Each speaker for a symposium gives an individual short speech about an aspect of the topic. Then, a question and answer forum will follow. There may be some dialogue among the team members in a symposium but the symposium is used as a means for an entire team to present information to an audience. The purpose is not to have a discussion among themselves.

Symposiums are used for public relations campaigns, team sales pitches, lectures, etc. Each speaker for a symposium should have a typed delivery outline in a portfolio. Memorization is fine but it's dangerous. If one person loses his or her memory, the entire team could be at risk for looking unprepared. Know your presentation. Each team member should memorize his or her introduction and conclusion; but it's not necessary to memorize entire speeches! **The team can have ONE running delivery outline with each member's part typed in the order he or she presents his or her subtopic; or members can have their own separate outlines**.

Tyler, Kristin and Dr. Finck prepare for a team symposium.
Photo Courtesy of Amber B. DuVentre

The Moderator

A moderator is strongly encouraged when there is a team symposium. An articulate and poised moderator can add credibility and organizational effectiveness. An ineffective moderator can make a decent presentation seem mediocre. Mediocrity is not an option! Therefore, embrace your "Godly greatness" by doing the following:

- Have a creative attention grabber. Don't just say, "Hi, welcome to this event." Grab the audience's attention and be creative and exciting!

- Introduce the team/organization's name and introduce yourself as the moderator

- Introduce the topic or the event theme

- Within the introduction, introduce the team members and their subtopics.

- Guide the symposium. Either stand up and re-introduce the speakers and their sub-topics one by one, make sure each speaker stands up in a timely fashion and re-introduces his or her subtopic, or make sure the speakers, one by one, introduce the next speaker and his/her sub-topic

- At the end of the symposium, but BEFORE the creative closure, thank the participants

- Summarize the main topic and the sub-topics

- End with a creative closure to make the session memorable

- Don't forget . . . If you are the speaker AND the moderator, you will have two creative attention grabbers and two creative closures. One attention grabber and one closure will be for the entire symposium. One attention grabber and one closure will be included in your solo presentation.

- **IF YOU HAVE A FORUM, YOU MUST HAVE A SECOND CLOSURE!!!**

Suggested Aids

The trend is the use of PowerPoint and multimedia devices. This is fine but please don't abuse the technology. An entire presentation with PowerPoint slides is not creative and overly utilized. It's best to use several types of aids especially for a sales/public relations' pitch. Showing a potential buyer that your team is versatile and flexible will be an advantage over a team that spends the entire presentation reading off a screen and pushing a remote control.

- Five to eight PowerPoint slides with pictures that are colorful and that emphasize your message, i.e., the living room, bedroom and bathroom of the timeshare you are trying to sell

- An object like a stuffed animal to show how your charity should be supported because so many children go without basic toys each year

- A pictogram that shows how student enrollment has increased in the area of Occupational Safety and Health Administration

A SAMPLE PREPARATION OUTLINE
for
The Team Symposium

TEAM INTRODUCTION (by the moderator)

I. We will not sell anything!
   (Attention grabber: emotional statement)

II. However, since you are approaching your sophomore year, and you are still undecided about a major, we wanted to inform you about the jobs you can get with a degree in organizational communication and why employers are drawn to graduates of this program. We are Team ABCD. I am Person D; and I am your moderator.
   (Introduce the team/organization's name, the topic/theme and the moderator)

III. The four of us have worked well together for three weeks to prepare and we decided that we don't want a hostile audience. So, you won't be subjected to high pressure tactics!
   (Tell why the team is qualified to speak and the benefits of listening)

IV. Person A will explain what you will encounter as an organizational communication major; Person B will tell you about the various jobs our graduates have; Person C will explain why employers are hiring our students over some other students who are in degree specific fields and I will . . . relax.

(Introduction of the team members and subtopics)

Image © Dean Mitchell, 2009. Used under license from Shutterstock, Inc.

MODERATOR'S TRANSITION: Person A. . . .don't you have something to say?

BODY

I. **PERSON A:** I certainly do. So you want to know what you can do with a degree that doesn't require you to sit for a state exam or collect 30 apprentice hours before actually getting a paycheck? Well, organizational communication teaches theories and skills that allow you to do anything. You will learn management techniques, leadership, training, presentation, and negotiation skills. You will learn how to handle conflict in the workplace or at any organization. You will learn strategies to effectively increase employee morale that should lead to an increase in productivity regardless of where you work. This is not a major for students who enjoy reading and listening to hour long lectures and then taking exams all semester. This major is for students who like to read, listen and then immediately apply what they have learned through individual and team projects. With this major, you have information and applications. Remember that.

MODERATOR: The next presenter will cover what it is like to major in Organizational Communication. . . . Hey Person B; do you remember all of that?

II. **PERSON B:** I certainly do. So you want to know what you can do with a degree in Organizational Communication? Our graduates are lawyers, Washington D.C. government officials, bank vice-presidents, professors, corporate trainers, human resource directors, business owners, ministers, executive directors for non-profit organizations, and the list goes on. We give you information about how to create strong relationships among employers and employees. We try to enhance your written and oral presentation skills. It doesn't matter what company you want to work for or what specific title you want to have. What matters is that you will be able to navigate through any training program for any company while having the special skills to help a company foster a healthier work environment. With this major, you can do anything! Remember that.

MODERATOR: Remember that. Person C . . .You have something to say too?

III. **PERSON C:** I certainly do. So you want to know why some employers specifically ask for our students? It's simple. Many graduates leave with the basic skills and knowledge about their respective fields. However, despite core knowledge, these students lack communication skills necessary to enhance employee morale. Many businesses are not as successful as they should be because employee morale is low or effective management practices are ignored or forgotten. Many companies want fresh ideas about how to solve problems and increase morale. This major teaches numerous theories about organizational structures and superior-subordinate relationships. Many companies would rather hire our students and give them company training rather than hire people who understand company policies but who lack an understanding of leadership principles, interpersonal communication and team dynamics. With this major, you dictate where you go and you can go anywhere. You're never stuck doing the same job because your skills and experiences are transferable. Remember that.

TEAM CONCLUSION (by the moderator)

MODERATOR: There's a lot to remember!

I. It has been a pleasure moderating for you. We are team ABCD. We thank you for being a great audience. We appreciate you.
(Indicate the end)

II. With a major in Organizational Communication you learn; you apply what you learn; you graduate with skills that are needed for every profession.
(Summarize your main points)

III. So, if nothing else . . . remember that.
(Creative closure: emotional statement)

MODERATOR: Are there any questions?

OPEN FORUM

QUESTION: Does your department help us to find jobs?

ANSWER: Yes. We post internship and job announcements. Many of our alumni call and request our students because they know the quality of education you will receive since they went through the program too.

QUESTION: Can you make a lot of money with this degree?

ANSWER: Well, as you heard, the jobs are quite diverse and several are considered high paying jobs. Most of our graduates don't start making $40 or $50 thousand a year but most wind up making that and much more within a few years of graduation.

MODERATOR: Are there any more questions? No?

SECOND CREATIVE CLOSURE

MODERATOR: All of us on this stage are passionate . . . passionate about Organizational Communication . . . passionate about education . . . and passionate in knowing how an education in Organizational Communication can create lucrative careers and enhance individual lives.

—Coel

***IF YOUR TEAM DOES NOT WANT TO HAVE A MODERATOR, THEN ONE TEAM MEMBER WILL STILL HAVE TO OPEN THE TEAM PRESENTATION WITH AN ATTENTION GRABBER FOLLOWED BY INTRODUCING HIMSELF/HERSELF, THE TEAM NAME/DEPARTMENT/ORGANIZATION, THE THEME/TOPIC, THE TEAM MEMBERS AND THEIR SUBTOPIC AREAS.

****WITH OR WITHOUT A MODERATOR, YOU <u>MUST</u> HAVE TRANSITIONS BETWEEN THE PRESENTERS. THE MODERATOR OR EACH TEAM MEMBER WILL NEED TO INTRODUCE THE NEXT PRESENTER AND HIS/HER SUBTOPIC: "JOHN WILL NOW TELL YOU ABOUT THE PITFALLS OF SMOKING." AFTER BEING INTRODUCED, ALWAYS SAY, "THANK YOU (NAME)" RIGHT BEFORE YOU PRESENT YOUR SUB-TOPIC AREA. EVERY PRESENTER SHOULD HAVE THE ELEMENTS OF AN INTRODUCTION AND ELEMENTS OF A CONCLUSION.

Rough Drafting Your Team Symposium Outline

MODERATOR'S INTRODUCTION

I. (Start with a question, quotation, short story, etc.)

  (Attention grabber)

II.

  (Introduce the team/organization's name, topic, and moderator/facilitator's name)

III.

  (Explain the benefits of listening)

IV.

  (Introduce the team members' names and subtopics)

  Moderator's transition into the 1st speaker:

Body

SPEAKER #1

(WRITE A FULL PREPARATION OUTLINE FOR AN INFORMATIVE OR PERSUASIVE PRESENTATION)

Moderator or team member's transition into the 2nd speaker

SPEAKER #2:

(WRITE A FULL PREPARATION OUTLINE FOR AN INFORMATIVE OR PERSUASIVE PRESENTATION)

Moderator or team member's transition into the 3rd speaker

SPEAKER #3

(WRITE A FULL PREPARATION OUTLINE FOR AN INFORMATIVE OR PERSUASIVE PRESENTATION)

Moderator or team member's transition into the 4th speaker

SPEAKER #4:

(WRITE A FULL PREPARATION OUTLINE FOR AN INFORMATIVE OR PERSUASIVE PRESENTATION)

Moderator or team member's transition into the Conclusion

MODERATOR'S CONCLUSION

I.

(Connect to the audience, thank the audience on behalf of the team or organization and indicate the end)

II.

(Summary of your main subtopics)

*REMEMBER: *Your summary of main points should be the subtopics introduced in IV. preview of the main points from the Introduction*

III. (Rhetorical question, refer back to the attention grabber, quotation, call to act, etc.)

(First Closure)

OPTIONAL FORUM

Moderator: Are there any questions?

MODERATOR'S REQUIRED SECOND CLOSURE (If there is a forum)

(Rhetorical question, refer back to the attention grabber, quotation, call to act, etc.)

If coherent, the audience will be thrilled to hear you speak! However, they will want you to be sentimental, brief and prepared. If you throw something together, the listeners won't be upset but they may talk about you on their way home.

Image © Lisa F. Young, 2009. Used under license from Shutterstock, Inc.

Toasts are social and business celebrations. The time of day is irrelevant and the location doesn't matter either. Sincerity is paramount.

You don't have to rehearse a lot. However, you do need to know what you will say. You don't need a delivery outline but you should create a preparation outline and be familiar with the organization of your presentation. If you stumble a lot, your own credibility will be affected and if you are at a business function, you could potentially embarrass yourself and your employer and co-workers.

Professor Patty S. Parish, M.S. has spent years educating students. Also, she and her husband are ministers who attend a lot of functions that require giving toasts. Her sample outline serves as a guide for those who wish to honor people with an organized and respectful toast presentation.

Suggested Aids

- A raised glass with a beverage in it
- A raised candle for a moment of silence or to light the room

---

A SAMPLE PREPARATION OUTLINE
for
The Toast

(The following is a fictitious Toast)

(WEDDING)

INTRODUCTION

I. Jacob and Lindsey are truly a storybook couple! My name is John and I have been given the great honor of giving this toast. I have been close friends with Jacob for many years and I have had the good fortune to watch the love between Jacob and Lindsey blossom and grow into something special. Tonight, we have gathered to celebrate that love.

(Attention grabber: emotional statement and why you are qualified to speak)

II. First of all, I would like to thank you on behalf of Jacob and Lindsey for coming and being a part of this very special night in their lives. Their joy and happiness is made complete by your presence tonight.

(Thank everyone for being a part of the celebration.)

III. Let's toast their fairy tale and their love.

(Preview the main points)

BODY

I. Jacob and Lindsey's relationship is truly one from the pages of a storybook.

   A. From the moment they met . . . that first glance from across the room . . . they knew that they were meant to be together. I was there and witnessed that glance!

    B. Their love is also like a fairy tale because they bring so much joy to each other every moment they are together. From the first time they were together, they found they had so much in common from baseball to a love of classical music.

    (First main point with support)

Transition: Their love deserves to have this toast.

  II. Let's raise our glasses and toast this special couple.

    A. Jacob and Lindsey, we toast you and your love. May your love always be like the sun . . . there to warm your days.

    B. May your love always be like the stars . . . there to enchant your nights.

    C. May your love always be like the moon . . . there to smile on all your hopes and dreams.

    D. Together . . . you're a dream come true.

    (Second main point with support)

CONCLUSION

  I. To Jacob and Lindsey . . .

    (Indicate the end)

  II. We salute your fairy tale which is your love!

    (Summarize your main points)

  III. We love you . . . cheers! Always remember what Elizabeth Browning said about love. "Love does not make the world go 'round; love is what makes the ride worthwhile."

    (Creative closures: emotional statements and a quotation)

Preparation outline submitted by:
Patty S. Parish, M.S.
Organizational Communication Lecturer
Basic Course Director
Murray State University

Rough Drafting Your Outline

INTRODUCTION

  I. (Start with a question, quotation, short story, etc.)

      (Attention grabber)

II.

      (Introduce the topic and why you are qualified to speak)

III.

      (Explain the benefits of listening)

IV.

      (Preview the main points)

Transition into the 1st main point:

Body

  I.

      A.

         1.

         2.

      B.

         1.

         2.

      (First main point with supporting material)

Transition into the 2nd main point:

    II.

        A.

        B.

           1.

           2.

        (Second main point with supporting material)

Transition into the 3rd main point:

    III.

        A.

           1.

           2.

        B.

           1.

           2.

CONCLUSION

    I.

        (Connect to the audience and indicate the end)

    II.

        (Summary of your main points)
        *REMEMBER: *Your summary of main points should be the same main points introduced in IV. preview of the main points from the Introduction*

    III. (End with a quotation, a rhetorical question, a call to act, a refer back to the attention grabber you said in I. of the introduction)

        (Creative Closure)

With the exception of on-site employees, most guests will know the honoree. Both genders are usually represented and the audience will reflect the occasion involving employment, family, community, etc. Regardless, the language in your message should be vivid and emotional to evoke a great love and remembrance of that person or concept.

Your delivery is so important if you pay tribute. A lackluster performance will minimize that person's achievements or that concept's power. You must have vocal variety and varied facial expressions. Sometimes tributes involve the media so be aware of any electronic devices and make sure you stand close enough to be heard and far enough away so that you don't sound like you are screaming into the microphone.

Suggested Aids

- A very large picture of the honoree but make sure it is tasteful, colorful and attractive

- A musical slideshow of memorable times in the life of the honoree

- Party favors and streamers at the end of your presentation to indicate a great celebration of the achievements of whatever or whomever you are celebrating

Image © Dimitri, 2009. Used under license from Shutterstock, Inc.

A SAMPLE PREPARATION OUTLINE
for
The Tribute

INTRODUCTION

I. It appeared to be an ordinary Fourth of July Celebration. But when he walked onto the stage, I noticed that he had the most amazing smile on his face and his skin was beautiful. I sat quietly as he spoke of his experiences during the Iraq War. He had lost his arm; he had lost his leg; he had lost his ability to dress himself in the morning. But as he spoke words of encouragement and wisdom and thankfulness, I noticed that he had not lost the one thing I took for granted each day . . . joy. He had not lost that inner peace . . . that inner joy.
(Attention grabber: short story)

II. I needed to share that I heard his testimony because we honor so many who have lost their lives. Today, we celebrate the strength of those who are left behind and the family members who love them. I have so many friends who have shared their pain with me. I know the pain is real.
(Introduce the topic and tell why you are qualified to speak)

III. So many of us have suffered a loss and even if we don't have a loved one in the Iraq War, we have battles we fight each day at work and in our homes.
(Explain the benefits of listening)

IV. A few minutes doesn't do them justice but I hope to give a glimpse of how much we appreciate who they are and who they will become.
(Preview the main points)

Transition: They leave home knowing who they represent.

BODY

I. United States Soldiers are special people. Soldiers know who they are. They are those willing to fight for humankind and for the goals set forth by our leaders.

(First main point with support)

A. They may be fearful, excited or confused, but regardless, they know that they will go out and defend democracy and freedom.

Transition: United States soldiers are amazing people.

II. Soldiers know they will become role models for so many who hear their stories or watch them live their lives.

(Second main point with support))

A. Those sitting with us tonight know that their experiences are a part of history that may be painful and yet liberating.

CONCLUSION

I. The war rages on . . . but so does the courage.

(Indicate the end)

II. So many are no longer with us and we grieve for their absence. But those who are still on this earth, sitting in this room, and watching through that camera . . . they are special and amazing because of who they are and who they will become.

(Summarize your main points)

III. We always honor the deceased but tonight we stand and salute the living souls and their families; we salute them for their strength; we salute them for their courage; we salute them for their love. Thank you United States soldiers and thank you family members for helping to keep their spirits high!

(Creative closure: emotional statements)

—Coel

Rough Drafting Your Outline

INTRODUCTION

I. (Start with a question, quotation, short story, etc.)

   (Attention grabber)

II.

   (Introduce the topic and why you are qualified to speak)

III.

   (Explain the benefits of listening)

IV.

   (Preview the main points)

   Transition into the 1st main point:

Body

I.

   A.

      1.

      2.

   B.

      1.

      2.

   (First main point with supporting material)

Transition into the 2nd main point:

   II.

        A.

        B.

          1.

          2.

        (Second main point with supporting material)

Transition into the 3rd main point:

   III.

        A.

          1.

          2.

        B.

          1.

          2.

CONCLUSION

   I.

        (Connect to the audience and indicate the end)

   II.

        (Summary of your main points)
        *REMEMBER: *Your summary of main points should be the same main points introduced in IV. preview of the main points from the Introduction*

   III. (End with a quotation, a rhetorical question, a call to act, a refer back to the attention grabber you said in I. of the introduction)

        (Creative Closure)

Forums are public **question and answer sessions**. Most forums bring anxiety to those who are subjected to them. No one wants to look silly in front of a lot of people and the fear of not knowing an answer to a question is stressful for many. However, if you remember that you are in front of people who think you have something important to share, and if you remember that there is no crime in not knowing an answer, then you will take some pressure off yourself.

If you are in a speaking situation, you must know something. Chances are, you even know more than most audience members. Therefore, all you have to do is answer their questions to the best of your ability.

If you don't know a specific answer:

- Let the person know you will investigate

- Take his or her phone number or email address

- Respond in a timely manner thus establishing credibility

I've heard people say that they find a speaker MORE credible even though they did not know an answer because that person took the time to find out the answer. It will show that not only are you knowledgeable about some things, but you have character and genuine concern for your audience.

Answering Questions With Ease and Poise

Former Adjunct professor, entrepreneur and motivational speaker Phil Bruschi, M.S., shares his *12 Deadly Sins* of presentational speaking in Chapter One. As a consultant for business presentations for over twenty years, he is an expert with forums. He is the author of the book *Mind Aerobics: The FundaMENTALS of Memory Fitness*. He taught Advanced Public Speaking at the University of North Carolina at Wilmington and provides tips for forums. He states:

The question and answer period following your presentation is an opportunity to continue meeting your presentation goals. Remember that a forum is still a part of your presentation, and, as such, you should take it seriously and prepare to be successful. Below are some tips and techniques that will ensure your success.

1. Try to anticipate the kinds of questions you will be asked and practice your answers ahead of time.

2. Always make eye contact with the individual asking the question while listening attentively. Make the same eye contact with the entire audience when you give your answers.

3. Remember to repeat the question aloud in case others did not hear the question asked.

4. There is no real need to compliment the individual on the question unless you are going to do it for everyone.

5. Ask "Do you have any questions?" instead of "What questions do you have?"

6. If you ask your audience a question, be sure to pause to give people enough time to think of their answers.

7. Continue to present yourself with the same effective presentation skills you had during your presentation with enough enthusiasm in volume while gesturing effectively, etc.

8. Take questions from the whole audience, not just from the same few people.

9. Whenever possible, try to use documented sources and credible data to support your answers.

10. Listen to each question with the same neutral nonverbal reactions and respond directly to the question.

11. If an individual continues to go on and on, be courteous, interrupt that person and ask if he or she has a question.

12. Keep your cool and remember to stay positive and professional. Do not show anger. You represent yourself, and if you are an employee you represent an organization.

Phil Bruschi, M.S.
Speaker/Author/Consultant
Mind and Memory Fitness Programs
Former Adjunct Professor of Communication
University of North Carolina at Wilmington

The Second Closure

After every forum, you must have a second closure. Most presenters do not complete their presentations correctly. Most end with, "Are there any other questions? Okay. Thank you for coming." It is rare for an audience to leave feeling inspired after a generic ending.

After the forum:

- Do not drag out an ending
- You already completed the full Conclusion with the three elements:
  1. indicating the end and thanking the audience
  2. summarizing
  3. creative closure
- Ask if there are other questions and when there are no more questions go straight into "The Second Closure"
- Whatever you do . . . do NOT end with "thank you!!!" Put the "thank you" in the FIRST element of the Conclusion and not after the closure or the second closure.

Image © AVAVA, 2009. Used under license fromShutterstock, Inc.

Overall, a presentation with or without a forum, can be amazing if time and effort are put into making it an informative/persuasive, exciting, and wonderful revelation of who you are!

Appendix

(SAMPLE) EVALUATION FORM
MONORE'S MOTIVATED SEQUENCE PERSUASIVE PRESENTATION

1A.) Grabbed Attention: Short Story/Rhetorical or Direct Question/Quotation/Emotional Statement or Action and had a preview of main points

1   2   3   4   5

1B.) Introduction was effectively delivered vocally, the eye contact was engaging and the body language was poised

1   2   3   4   5

2A.) Did you show the need: concise statement of the problem followed by statistics, examples OR did you go right into what we should do?

1   2   3   4   5

2B.) Did you tell us how the problem affects us before offering the solution?

1   2   3   4   5

2C.) Was your vocal delivery effective during the need step? (volume, vocal variety, rate, pauses etc.)

1   2   3   4   5

2D.) Was your visual delivery effective during the need step? (eye contact, use of controlled gestures, body language)

1   2   3   4   5

3A.) Did you satisfy the need by providing additional credible support that included dates? (examples, statistics, etc.) Did they have value?

1   2   3   4   5

3B.) Was your vocal delivery during the satisfaction step effective?

1   2   3   4   5

3C.) Was your visual delivery effective during the satisfaction step?

1   2   3   4   5

4.) Did you kill the objections at the right place and were your vocal and visual deliveries strong during the objections?

1   2   3   4   5

5A.) Did you visualize by telling us what would or would not happen?

1   2   3   4   5

5B.) Were your vocal and verbal deliveries effective during the visualization step?

1   2   3   4   5

6A.) Did you call for action, summarize and have a creative closure without having multiple conclusions?

1   2   3   4   5

6B.) Was your delivery effective during the action step? Was your eye contact prolonged? Did you use effective pauses?

1   2   3   4   5

7A.) Did you use an appropriate visual aid or did you throw it into the presentation? (Was it large enough/did it aid the presentation?)

1   2   3   4   5

7B.) Was your delivery effective when you displayed your presentation aid? (posture, appropriate gesturing, movement of the aid, etc.)

1   2   3   4   5

8.) Was the time limit met? (5–7 minutes)

3   4   5   6   7   8   9   10

9.) Did you use excessive ums, ahs, mispronunciations, throat clearing and coughing throughout this presentation?

3   4   5   6   7   8   9   10

Delivery Outline:

1   2   3   4   5   6   7   8   9   10

Preparation Outline followed the book and MY instructions:

0   25   26   27   28   29   30   31   32   33   34   35   36   37   38   39   40

—*Coel*

STUDENT'S NAME: _____

COURSE TITLE: _____

INSTRUCTOR'S NAME: _____ TOTAL _____ OUT OF 150 POINTS

(SAMPLE) EVALUATION FORM
PROBLEM-SOLUTION OR CAUSE-EFFECT PERSUASIVE PRESENTATION

1A.) Grabbed attention: short story/rhetorical or direct question/quotation/ emotional statement or action and had a preview of main points

1   2   3   4   5

1B.) Introduction was effectively delivered vocally, the eye contact was engaging and the body language was poised

1   2   3   4   5

2A.) Did you state the problem or cause followed by statistics, examples OR did you go right into what we should do?

1   2   3   4   5

2B.) Did you tell us how the problem or cause affects us before offering the solution or effects?

1   2   3   4   5

2C.) Was your vocal delivery effective while stating the problem or cause? (volume, vocal variety, rate, pauses etc.)

1   2   3   4   5

2D.) Was your visual delivery effective while stating the problem or cause? (eye contact, use of controlled gestures, body language)

1   2   3   4   5

2E.) Did you provide credible support that was cited properly and did the support include dates? (examples, statistics,, etc.) Did they have value?

1   2   3   4   5

3A.) Did you offer solutions or effects?

1   2   3   4   5

3B.) Was your vocal delivery effective while stating the solutions or effects? (volume, vocal variety, rate, pauses etc.)

1   2   3   4   5

3C.) Was your visual delivery effective while stating the solutions or effects? (eye contact, use of controlled gestures, body language)

1   2   3   4   5

3D.) Did you provide more credible support that was cited properly and included dates? (examples, statistics, etc.) Did they have value?

1   2   3   4   5

4A.) Did your conclusion have a clear indication of the end, a summary and a creative closure without having multiple conclusions?

1   2   3   4   5

4B.) Was your delivery effective during the conclusion? Was your eye contact prolonged? Did you use effective pauses?

1   2   3   4   5

5A.) Did you use an appropriate aid or did you throw it into the presentation? (Was it appropriate and large enough? Did it **aid** the presentation?)

1   2   3   4   5

5B.) Was your delivery effective when you displayed your presentation aid? (posture, appropriate gesturing, movement of the aid, etc.)

1   2   3   4   5   6   7   8   9   10

6.)   Was the time limit met? (5–7 minutes)

                          3   4   5   6   7   8   9   10

7.)   Did you use excessive ums, ahs, mispronunciations, throat clearing and coughing throughout this presentation?

                          3   4   5   6   7   8   9   10

Delivery Outline:

1   2   3   4   5   6   7   8   9   10

Preparation Outline followed the book and MY instructions:

0   25   26   27   28   29   30   31   32   33   34   35   36   37   38   39   40

—Coel

STUDENT'S NAME: _____

COURSE TITLE: _____

INSTRUCTOR'S NAME: _____

(SAMPLE) EVALUATION FORM
DYADIC INTERPERSONAL OR TEAM PRESENTATION

50 POINTS TEAM GRADE   50 POINTS INDIVIDUAL GRADE

ORGANIZATION OF THE ENTIRE PRESENTATION

Presentation was clear and had a noticeable structure

Presentation was creative and professional

Presentation was obviously not thrown together the night before

Met content requirements

14   15   16   17   18   19   20   21   22   23   24   25

CONTENT AND DELIVERY OF INDIVIDUAL PRESENTATIONS

Presentations were well-structured and met the required time limit

Presenters were fluent in their verbal deliveries and they did not excessively stumble or use vocal fillers like "ah-um," throat clearing, smacking, "you know" or "like" etc.

Presenters had controlled body movements and effectively used planned and natural gestures

Presenters had appropriate eye contact and used minimal notes

Presenters used appropriate presentation aids and the usage was effective and engaging

Presenters looked professional

Forums were conducted well and presenters were poised when answering questions (if needed)

6   7   8   9   10   11   12   13   14   15

THE MINIMUM REQUIREMENTS WERE MET

Hit the 15–20 minute overall time limit

All individual presentations were within the stipulated time limit

Presentation Aids were appropriate, large enough, clear enough, and they reflected the rules for fonts and color

Preparation and Delivery Outlines were handed in on time

Presentation outlines were in a folder or portfolio

1   2   3   4   5   6   7   8   9   10

TEAM PRESENTATION TOTAL _____ out of 50 points

—Coel

NAME: _____

DUE DATE: _____ at the BEGINNING of the Class

TEAM MEMBER EVALUATION = 25 points maximum

*Circle the number that most represents that person's contribution to the team's success in that category.

Make sure you add up the total amount of points and place the score on the blank line.

6 is poor   7 is average   8 is good   9 is very good   10 is excellent

Team Member's Name _____

1. Had respect for team members (attending the meetings on time, concentrating and not taking phone calls and text messages, not whispering during meetings, being alert and productive, used respectful language, actually comprehensively listened to others

                                                                    5   6   7   8   9   10

2. Completed his or her individual assignments well and on time

                              7   8   9   10   11   12   13   14   15

                  Total Score out of 25 _____

Team Member's Name _____

1. Had respect for team members (attending the meetings on time, concentrating and not taking phone calls and text messages, not whispering during meetings, being alert and productive, used respectful language, actually comprehensively listened to others

                                                                     5   6   7   8   9   10

2. Completed his or her individual assignments well and on time

                              7   8   9   10   11   12   13   14   15

                  Total Score out of 25 _____

Team Member's Name _____

1. Had respect for team members (attending the meetings on time, concentrating and not taking phone calls and text messages, not whispering during meetings, being alert and productive, used respectful language, actually comprehensively listened to others

                                                                     5   6   7   8   9   10

2. Completed his or her individual assignments well and on time

                              7   8   9   10   11   12   13   14   15

                  Total Score out of 25 _____

Team Member's Name _____

1. Had respect for team members (attending the meetings on time, concentrating and not taking phone calls and text messages, not whispering during meetings, being alert and productive, used respectful language, actually comprehensively listened to others

                                                                     5   6   7   8   9   10

2. Completed his or her individual assignments well and on time

                              7   8   9   10   11   12   13   14   15

                  Total Score out of 25 _____